# CLOSER
# TO THE
# TRUTH

## JEWISH, CHRISTIAN,
## & MUSLIM PERSPECTIVES ON
# ABRAHAMIC SACRIFICE

ISBN: 978-1-59784-957-9
Ebook: 978-1-59784-993-7

Published by Tughra Books
www.tughrabooks.com
335 Clifton Ave. Clifton New Jersey 07011

TUGHRA BOOKS

# CLOSER
# TO THE

# TRUTH

## JEWISH, CHRISTIAN,
## & MUSLIM PERSPECTIVES ON
# ABRAHAMIC SACRIFICE

Albert Frolov - M. Fethullah Gülen - Heidi Hoover - Paul Jacobson
Serdar Kilic - Anne McRae Wrede - Yakov Nagen - Daniel Skubik
Sumeyra Tosun - Mariya Tytarenko - Hakan Yesilova

# CONTENTS

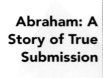

# CLOSER TO THE TRUTH

## INTRODUCTION

The Festival of Sacrifice (Eid al-Adha) is one of the two most important celebrations in the Islamic tradition. About two months following the end of Ramadan fasting and festivity (Eid al-Fitr), Muslims around the world join in prayer and feasting again for Eid al-Adha. Those who can afford distribute meat of sacrificial animals to the poor and neighbors during this eid which also marks one of the biggest annual assemblies of the world: the Hajj – the pilgrimage. Millions of Muslims flock in Mecca to observe the rites of the Hajj, pray at the holiest sanctuary of Islam, the Ka'ba, and honor Prophet Abraham, who, Muslims believe, built it. They remember Hagar and Ishmael as they walk about and drink from the well.

As featured in this work, Prophet Abraham's story is almost identical in many ways in Judaism, Christianity, and Islam, and full of lessons for the faithful across traditions. Abraham symbolizes matchless submission and trust in God, spirit of sacrifice, and generous hospitality. His is the path to get closer to the Truth; this is what Abrahamic sacrifice (*qurban*) stands for.

OUR EGO, OUR "I," IS AN ILLUSORY, SPECULATIVE NON-ENTITY THAT ALWAYS STRIVES TO PASS ITSELF OFF AS THE MOST "REAL" ENTITY, AS SOMETHING THAT CAN LORD IT OVER EVERYTHING IN EXISTENCE.

# TEST OF THE MOST MERCIFUL

## by Albert Frolov

*Qurban,* as translated from classic Arabic, means "approaching," or "drawing closer." In due course, the word has appropriated a different, metaphorical meaning—"sacrifice(ing)." So, as any metaphor within a phrase usually relates to the direct, original meaning of this phrase, "sacrifice(ing)," too, relates to "drawing closer" – drawing closer, of course, to the Divine.

Indeed, *Qurban* is an integral part of the very name of an annual Muslim holiday. It connotes a deep meaning of "Islam" (i.e., a loving, self-surrender to God) and conveys the latter's metaphysical pathos, for it literally says, "If you want to draw nearer to Him, make a sacrifice!" And why not sacrifice, if everything already belongs only to Him? It's not a sacrifice; it's one's detachment from something that one does not really own, something that is His. It's also something connoting a fundamental meaning of monotheism, something that is reflected in the richness of the Russian language when they say, "God gives it, and God takes it away." Why are we then sad if we're giving back a thing that we never really owned?

If we think further, we realize that the Creator brings about everything around us and possesses full ownership of it and that we actually own nothing: neither the houses where we live, nor the cars we drive, nor even our bodies, nor even the soul that is who we really are. In the same way, we cannot lay claim to our beloved ones, sons or daughters... Nor can we exert any patronage over them. We badly want to, but we cannot. We mistakenly assume that we must exert at least *some* ownership or patronage toward something directly related to us (e.g., ourselves and our closest ones). It seems as if this is how our human essence and human nature should be. Alas, these wishes are nothing but whimsical. They are just another ridiculous excuse for our Ego, our "I," an illusory, speculative non-entity that always strives to pass itself off as the most "real" entity, as something that can lord it over everything in existence [1]. We are the creations of God, and everything around us and everything inside us belongs only to Him. We own nothing.

Our "I" was given to us for only one purpose: to abstract, and fully distinguish ourselves, from other objects (this is something only humans can do). When one realizes that everything belongs to one God and is constantly created and controlled by His Divine Wisdom and Power, when one sees the Hand of the All-Powerful God at work right within oneself, one experiences the spiritual state of *hayrah* (an extreme degree of surprise and amazement). One stands still, immersed in awe, and then falls down on the prayer carpet, not daring to raise his or her head as they witness the Divine reflections of the names of the Lord, with which everything around and inside him appears embroiled. This person will have a lump in the throat, for sometimes one feels uncomfortable because of one's inability to adequately thank even other people for their relatively small service for us, let along being able to thank God. One's total inability to thank the One who endows us these fantastic gifts for our temporary use will forever leave a bitter feeling in the heart of a servant. Henceforth, this servant of God will carry the banner of faith throughout his life and sacrifice all that he or she can on this path, just as Prophet Abraham did.

Abraham, one of the greatest prophets, underwent many trials: his own people tried to burn him alive only because he believed in one Creator, and he was forced to leave them for good. Abraham made a very important request of the Almighty: "Oh, my Lord! Give me those who will be of the righteous people [i.e., an offspring]" [2]. The Holy Qur'an tells what follows: "When he reached maturity and began to help his father, Abraham said: 'Oh, son! Verily, I see in my dream that I am slaughtering you!'" "When he reached maturity" means that Ismael was on the verge of entering an adult life, in which a father's wisdom would be of help and when the prophet's attachment to him reached its apogee.

This dream was a direct order from the Almighty to sacrifice his only son, a long-awaited gift from the Almighty.

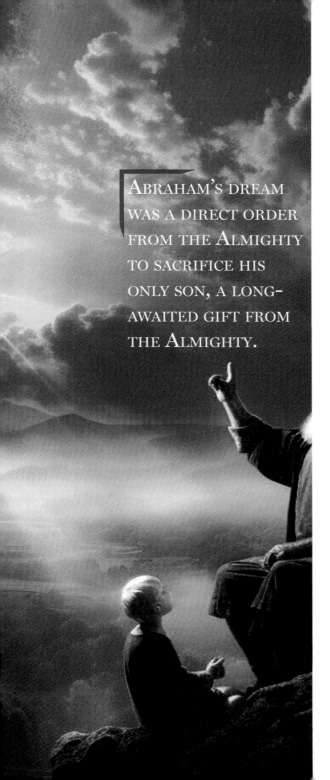

ABRAHAM'S DREAM WAS A DIRECT ORDER FROM THE ALMIGHTY TO SACRIFICE HIS ONLY SON, A LONG-AWAITED GIFT FROM THE ALMIGHTY.

And prophetic dreams are always accurate—even in their dreams, there is no place for lies or distortion of reality) [3]. "Look at this case, tell me *your* opinion," continued Abraham.

Sacrificing oneself on the path of God? For the prophet's son, as young as he was (probably around thirteen years old), sacrificing himself out of obedience to a divine command proved not so difficult. He only said: "O my dear father! Do as you are commanded. You will find me, by God's will, one of those who show steadfast patience." By that time, this boy (according to most Islamic sources, it was Ismael not Isaac) was Abraham's only son, the apple of his eye.

*"Then when both had submitted to God's will, and Abraham had laid him down on the side of his forehead."*

Indeed, Abraham (peace be upon him) was a prophet, but he was also a man, a man with his own "I." Ephemeral, weak, and unreal, but still "I." The soul of Abraham shuddered and whispered to him that his son was part of his flesh, that he had some right over him... The boy, in turn, knew that, if his father saw his face, he would pity him. So, he asked his father to turn him face down ... [4]. But the prophetic light is so great that it overshadows everything ephemeral and unreal. The prophet's hand, guided by a prophetic spirit, did not tremble. Even though Abraham turned his son face down, he couldn't disobey an order of the Almighty. If God orders something, then, therefore, in this lies its own wisdom, its own mercy. "And We called him: 'O, Abraham! You were sincere about your dream! Indeed, this is how we reward those who do good! Truly, this is a clear test! And we redeemed him with a large sacrificial animal.'"

Muslims may ponder these realities when they sacrifice an animal on Eid al-Adha. The Creator of all things does not demand they sacrifice themselves or their sons or daughters but simply obliges them to buy a lamb and share it with the poor–and even this, on the condition that they are wealthy enough: give a third to the needy, eat a third, and keep a third in reserve, if they wish so—an eminently reasonable demand! [5]

Afterward, God even rewards us for our sacrifice. Indeed, the sacrificial ram (or cow) will adorn our tables and delight our stomachs, as well as being a consolation for the poor.

*Qurban* is also associated with the notion of "Eid," the latter being the Arabic word for "holiday." During Eid, the spirit of sacrifice and readiness to give away comes is replaced, thanks to a

command of the Almighty, by the spirit of joy. Meals are cooked on stoves, and houses become full of the cheerful noise of guests. The Prophet, the man who was responsible for conveying the universal message of God to all the people, and who would frequently weep for the sake of people's salvation, enjoyed this holiday and ensured that other people enjoyed it as well. He said that in the message he brought "... there is room [for fun and joy] and that I was sent with the religion of tolerance and gentleness" [6]. Indeed, Eid al-Adha is a holiday for both the soul and body. It is an easy test that is followed by an important reward, worldly and otherworldly. In this sense, our whole life can become an endless *Qurban*.

## Notes

1. Bediuzzaman Said Nursi, *The Words* (the Thirtieth Word), p. 552, New Jersey, 2005.
2. 100-107 Qur'anic verses of the Chapter "Saffat" are used here and in the following texts.
3. Abu al-Qasim az-Zamakhshari, *al-Kashaf fi haqaik at-tanzil wa uyun al-akauil fi ujuh at-ta'wil*, Egypt, 2000, v. 3, p. 687.
4. Ibid, p. 689.
5. Opinion of the majority of Muslim jurists (al-Said al-Sabiq, *Fiqh as-Sunna*, Cairo, 1999, t.3, p. 192).
6. Ibid.

ALBERT FROLOV, PHD, IS A LECTURER AT RESPECT GRADUATE SCHOOL IN PENNSYLVANIA.

He prescribed for you the same religion He enjoined upon Noah, and what We inspired to you, and what We enjoined upon Abraham, and Moses, and Jesus: "You shall uphold the religion, and be not divided therein."

ASH-SHURA 42:13

# SACRIFICE
## A MEANS OF BECOMING CLOSER TO GOD

### by M. Fethullah Gülen

At the beginning of the second chapter of the Qur'an, God Almighty declares that He is the actual owner of things and we are temporary keepers: *"Out of what We have provided for them they spend..."* Namely, what we donate is actually nothing but blessings He has granted us. By pointing out that "He" is the actual Provider of sustenance, He reminds us that there is no need for us to worry about depletion. This point is more directly expressed in another verse, that God Almighty, the Omnipotent One, is the Provider of sustenance of all creatures (Dhariyat 51:58).

A person supporting others with their personal wealth—be it in the form of alms or sacrificial meat—is the minimal degree of generosity for one who considers himself or herself a believer.

As for the maximum degree of helping others, let us ponder over the following verse:

*"They (believers) prefer [others] over themselves, even though poverty be their own lot."* (Hashr 59:9)

Someone who acts with this spirit will offer their time, knowledge, wisdom, wealth, and vision—in short, God's every bestowal—to the utmost degree and will share what they have with others.

This festival is not only an act of worship observed individually. It is a time when believers conquer hearts in different parts of the world by generously sharing the meat of their sacrifice with others.

The noble Prophet said that for those who observe this good act, God will render their sacrifices given away for His sake into steeds to ride with on the Day of Judgment, when they are most needy. Then, as they will fill with feelings of admiration and wonder, they will try to decide which one to ride.

The noble Prophet demanded everybody who can afford it to offer a sacrifice, and scholars of the Hanafi school ruled that it is no less necessary (*wajib*) than *zakat* alms for the wealthy. Those who have the means should not forget the fact that poorer ones have a right to benefit from their wealth.

**Provisions for the Hereafter**
Another Qur'anic verse encourages people to donate from what they love:

*"You will never be able to attain godliness and virtue until you spend of what you love (in God's cause or to provide sustenance for the needy)"* (Al Imran 3:92).

Thus, it is advised to choose the sacrificial animal from healthy, robust ones with no physical defect, for it will become a steed on the way to Paradise. Note that everything done here will appear to us in the Hereafter with their true reflection of their meaning. As we cannot know how things will be in the next world, we cannot really imagine in what form they will return to us. Maybe our sacrificial animals will appear before us like a plane, ship, boat, or a good horse in the next life. If we consider the issue with respect to the immensity of God's graces and the truthfulness of His promises, we can say that they will definitely return to us somehow.

According to a report by our mother Aisha, God's Messenger distributed two thirds of the animal he sacrificed to the poor and left the remaining third at home for his family. This is the criterion for one who wishes to distribute the meat in compliance with the example of the Prophet.

As a matter of fact, seeking closeness to God in all acts of worship, saying "O God, I did this for Your sake only," and having due integrity in one's feelings must be the basis of our actions. When giving from one's wealth—to which we feel much attached—it is necessary to remember other things one can possibly give and show obedience to Divine orders. During the festival of sacrifice, we remember the situation of Prophet Abraham and his son, who grasped so well the gist of worship and submission to Divine orders, when they were tested with the greatest sacrifice one can possibly make: *"Then when both had submitted to God's will, and Abraham had laid him down on the side of his forehead"* (as-Saffat 37:103).

If a believer begins the worship of sacrifice with such intention from the very beginning, then all of their ensuing acts will be counted as worship and other things done for the sake of this good deed will also return to that person as rewards in the Hereafter.

When the truth of our seemingly small actions is revealed to us in the Hereafter, they will make us say in astonishment, "O God, how bountiful You are! You have taken these little things, made them bloom, flourish, transform, become eternal, and now You are offering them to us!" In this respect, a person should fulfill the worship of sacrifice in this world with an inner feeling of richness and contentment of the heart. The following verse also refers to this fact:

*"(Bear in mind that) neither their flesh nor their blood reaches God, but only piety and consciousness of God reach Him from you"* (al-Hajj 22:37).

If a person carries out this act of worship by viewing it as a connection with God Almighty and a chance to be rewarded by Him, then that person will meet very different riches and surprises in the next world.

M. FETHULLAH GÜLEN IS AN ISLAMIC SCHOLAR AND THE AUTHOR OF
*MUHAMMAD: THE MESSENGER OF GOD.*

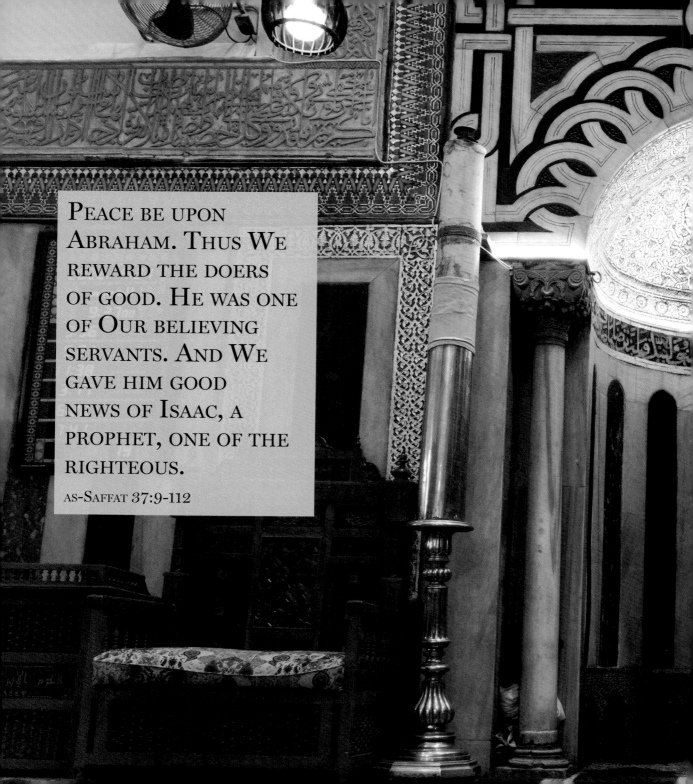

PEACE BE UPON ABRAHAM. THUS WE REWARD THE DOERS OF GOOD. HE WAS ONE OF OUR BELIEVING SERVANTS. AND WE GAVE HIM GOOD NEWS OF ISAAC, A PROPHET, ONE OF THE RIGHTEOUS.

AS-SAFFAT 37:9-112

*Ibrahimi Mosque in the ancient city of Hebron.*

# ABRAHAM

## & HIS RELATIONSHIP WITH GOD

### by Rabbi Heidi Hoover

Jews refer to Abraham as Avraham Avinu, Abraham our father. He is very important to us: he is our first patriarch, the one whose family was chosen to have a covenant with God. Of course, not all Jews believe the same things about our spiritual ancestors, whose stories are told in our Torah. I will share the way I think about Abraham, with which many, but not all, Jews would probably agree.

It is not important, to me, to think of Abraham as perfect in any way. Rather, I see him as just as human as any one of us, and that is meaningful to me, because if Abraham was an imperfect human, and God chose him, it means God can choose us, too. One of the stories we learn about Abraham is that God told him that He, God, was going to destroy the great cities of Sodom and Gomorrah because of the evil behavior of the people there. Abraham does not simply accept this. He argues on behalf of any righteous people who may live there. He stands up to God, asking whether God will destroy the place if as few as 10 righteous people live there. God says no – though apparently there were not even 10, because the place is destroyed (Genesis, 18:17-33).

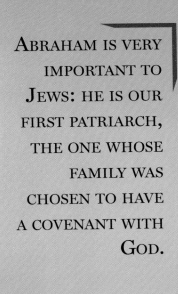

ABRAHAM IS VERY IMPORTANT TO JEWS: HE IS OUR FIRST PATRIARCH, THE ONE WHOSE FAMILY WAS CHOSEN TO HAVE A COVENANT WITH GOD.

Later, God commands Abraham to sacrifice his son Isaac (Yitzchak), and Abraham does not object at all (Genesis, 22:1-19). This is troubling for many Jews, who struggle with how a father could agree to sacrifice his son, regardless of who is telling him to. When we find the behavior of our patriarchs and matriarchs troubling, we see it as an invitation to look more deeply at the story to find meaning for our own lives.

One of the ways I have understood Abraham's lack of objection is that it's easier sometimes to stand up for strangers, as Abraham stood up for the people of Sodom and Gomorrah, than to stand up for ourselves. This is a reading that sees Abraham as being so devastated by the command to sacrifice Isaac that he numbly complies without argument. (Jews also understand the stories in our Torah as having multiple meanings, even contradictory ones.) This interpretation helped me to understand something about many people, not just Abraham.

We look to Avraham Avinu to find God's first covenant with a family that later became the Jewish people. We look to him as an example of a relationship with God—he tries to understand, he questions, he argues, sometimes he looks out for himself, and sometimes he does as he is told. He isn't perfect, but God chooses him. And we can strive to have that kind of relationship with God, too.

HEIDI HOOVER SERVES AS THE RABBI OF TEMPLE BETH EMETH V'OHR PROGRESSIVE SHAARI ZEDEK IN BROOKLYN

# ABRAHAM

## & HIS LOVING HOSPITALITY

### by Paul Jacobson

The introduction of Abram in the twelfth chapter of the biblical book of Genesis, aids in the Hebrew Bible's transition from a text focused on the general workings of the world, to a text specifically focused on the creation, development, and flourishing of the Israelite people and nation. God calls upon Abram to leave his land, his birthplace, and his father's home in Ur of the Chaldeans (in the Mesopotamian region) and go on a journey "to the land that God will show him" (Genesis 12:1-2). That Abram followed such a call with such deeply trusting faith is quite remarkable.

As a result of Abram's faithful journey, God chooses to establish a covenant with him. Renaming Abram as Abraham, God promises Abraham that he will "become a father of the multitude of nations," that Abraham's descendants will be "exceedingly numerous," and that Abraham and his offspring will live in the land of Canaan as an "everlasting possession" (Genesis 17:4-8). As a partner with God in this covenant, Abraham and his descendants must keep God's commandments, and males will be circumcised as an indication of their adherence to God's covenant.

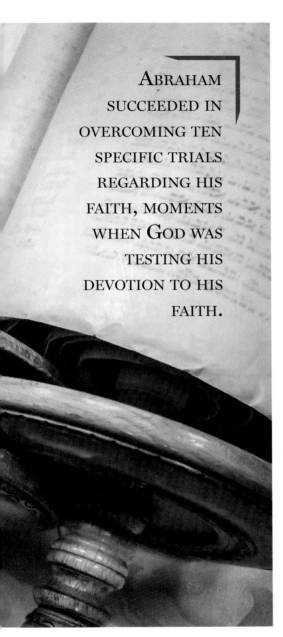

ABRAHAM SUCCEEDED IN OVERCOMING TEN SPECIFIC TRIALS REGARDING HIS FAITH, MOMENTS WHEN GOD WAS TESTING HIS DEVOTION TO HIS FAITH.

In addition to the establishment of the covenant, Abraham's character is developed in other scenes. We see Abraham as a man who cares deeply for his family and for the needs of others. In one remarkable episode, when God announces to Abraham the destruction of the cities of Sodom and Gomorrah, Abraham questions God directly, demanding that the Judge of the world act righteously. More gently, Abraham is regarded as a person of loving hospitality, welcoming three strangers into his tent, and feeding them, when he himself is recovering from having just circumcised himself. He also faces the tremendous trial of being called by God to bring forward his beloved son Isaac as a sacrifice – until an angel of God intervenes. Teachings from rabbinic sages developed concepts surrounding Abraham's unbreakable, unwavering faith in God, and that during his lifetime, he succeeded in overcoming ten specific trials regarding his faith, moments when God was testing his devotion to his faith.

Abraham is remembered in our daily prayers, traditionally recited three times a day. The opening prayer of a rubric in our service known as the *Amidah*, the "standing" prayer, is an extended reference to our patriarchs (and in egalitarian congregations to our matriarchs too). We praise God as the "God of Abraham, God of Isaac, and God of Jacob" linking ourselves today with our biblical ancestors. Such an important historical connection inspires the Jewish people to aspire to a life in which we live by the best attributes of our ancestors, and continue to make those values our own.

PAUL JACOBSON, A PSYCHOTHERAPIST/COUNSELLOR BASED IN SYDNEY, AUSTRALIA, SERVED AS A RABBI FOR MANY YEARS IN THE US.

"O MY FATHER,
DO AS YOU ARE
COMMANDED;
YOU WILL FIND ME,
GOD WILLING,
ONE OF THE
STEADFAST."

AS-SAFFAT 37:102

*Maqam Ibrahim - the Station of
Abraham, in the Masjid al-Haram
in Mecca.*

بِسْمِ اللهِ الرَّحْمٰنِ الرَّحِيمِ

# SUBMISSION

## by Serdar Kilic

Among the plethora of events and miracles in the life of Prophet Muhammad ﷺ, there is one that was particularly unique. Around a year before the Muslim community's migration to Medina, the Prophet ﷺ was taken by a heavenly steed from Mecca to Jerusalem, and from there lifted to the seven heavens. At the end of this journey, he was brought to the direct presence of God, closer than anyone before or after him.

One of the many fruits of this stunning occasion is the revelation of the last two verses of chapter al-Baqarah in the Qur'an. Because they were revealed to the Prophet ﷺ from God without any intermediary, they are considered to hold a unique degree of importance compared to the rest of the scripture. Just these two verses hold enough meaning for volumes of scholarship; nevertheless, if we wanted to summarize their contents, we could say that they contain a summary of the true nature of a believer.

Within these descriptions is one that conveys a concept oft-mentioned in the whole Book: submission and obedience. As it announces succinctly: "And the believers say: We hear and We obey" [2:285]:

وَقَالُواْ سَمِعْنَا وَأَطَعْنَا

This proclamation perfectly encapsulates the psych0-spiritual state of the believer. When the Divine Command comes, he accepts it unconditionally and applies it entirely. The reality of God's Lordship is that He has the unqualified right to command his property as He wills; and the reality of our servanthood is that we must obey the Divine Injunction with complete deference.

Defiance to a command is the sign of rebellion, and its acceptance a mark of submission. In our mundane lives, we naturally exhibit this understanding, from the orders of a supervisor to the commands of a national leader. This principle applies just as well to our relationship with God. In whatever we do, failing to meet the standards of morality and obedience to the Divine Law reflects our inner nature. One that does not manifest perfection but is twisted and disfigured into pure monstrousness.

It is for this reason that the prophets, blessings upon them all, are necessarily free of sin or disobedience. Their role as guides and role models for the believers entails that they must themselves be pure examples of what God wants us to be like. The life of every single prophet is filled with examples of their utmost submission to the Divine Command. This is seldom more obvious than in the explication of a particular event in the life of Prophet Abraham.

Prophet Abraham had already gone through many trials throughout his life. In trying to guide his father, he was disowned and hated. In trying to guide his people away from misguidance and idol worship, he was persecuted and thrown into a raging fire. Despite all of that, his resilience and strength in belief had stayed strong. However, his greatest test would only be made clear at a later time.

There are many things that a person values, forming a hierarchy within their mind and heart. Be it money, family, or a loved one, there are a plethora of things that our faith in God can be tested by. Undoubtedly, however, the most terrifying trial that one can experience is that of a parent being tested by their beloved child. And this is exactly what lay in wait for Prophet Abraham.

One night, Prophet Abraham saw a dream, a true source of revelation for prophets; in it, he was commanded to sacrifice the life of his precious son Ismail. When he woke from his dream, he did so with a heavy task on his shoulders. This is the first part of the formula as mentioned in the verse above: to hear of the command and accept its significance. Right after, Prophet Abraham went to his son and informed him of what the Lord of the Worlds had ordered him to do.

What happened next is a reinforcement of the proper response to God's mandates. Though Ismail was just a young boy with a full life ahead, his response was even more immediate and enthusiastic than his father's, as he hoped to console him by reminding him of the proper path. His words are beautifully expressed in the Qur'an: "Abraham said:

'O my dear son! I have seen in a dream that I must sacrifice you. So tell me what you think.' He replied, 'O my dear father! Do as you are commanded. If God wishes, you will find me steadfast'" [37:102].

قَالَ يَبُنَىَّ إِنِّى أَرَىٰ فِي ٱلْمَنَامِ أَنِّي أَذْبَحُكَ فَانظُرْ مَاذَا تَرَىٰ قَالَ يَأَبَتِ افْعَلْ مَا تُؤْمَرُ سَتَجِدُنِي إِن شَاءَ اللّٰهُ مِنَ الصَّٰبِرِينَ

Here we see the second and most important part of the formula in the Chapter: to obey the command without reference to deception or treachery. And this is precisely what Prophet Abraham and his son displayed, by laying the young man down and attempting to follow through on the act.

When Prophet Abraham showed his formidable resolve in submitting to the Divine Command, God called down to him, declaring that He rescinded his order and that the whole occasion was a trial with the sole purpose of revealing their true characters, that of true believers in complete submission.

In reward, God sent down a ram from the heavens, instructing that they sacrifice it instead. This entire trial was without a doubt the most harrowing decision Prophet Abraham had to undertake, and one that represented his unmatched obedience. It is in commemoration of this event that Muslims make their own animal sacrifices every year on Eid Al-Adha, to celebrate and raise the flag of submission that Prophet Abraham first did millennia ago.

The ending of Prophet Abraham's ordeal was also a perfect reflection of the ending state of the true submissive believer, one that is blessed and exalted by God. In being saved from having to sacrifice his precious child, the story perfectly encapsulates the ending of Chapter al-Baqarah, a plea sent to the Lord of the Worlds that He bestow on us his Mercy and Grace: "God does not burden any soul more than it can bear. All good will be for its own benefit, and all evil will be to its own loss. The believers pray: 'Our Lord! Do not punish us if we forget or make a mistake. Our Lord! Do not place a burden on us like the one you placed on those before us. Our Lord! Do not burden us with what we cannot bear. Pardon us, forgive us, and have mercy on us'" [2:286].

لَا يُكَلِّفُ اللّٰهُ نَفْسًا إِلَّا وُسْعَهَا لَهَا مَا كَسَبَتْ وَعَلَيْهَا مَا اكْتَسَبَتْ رَبَّنَا لَا تُؤَاخِذْنَا إِن نَّسِينَا أَوْ أَخْطَأْنَا رَبَّنَا وَلَا تَحْمِلْ عَلَيْنَا إِصْرًا كَمَا حَمَلْتَهُ عَلَى الَّذِينَ مِن قَبْلِنَا رَبَّنَا وَلَا تُحَمِّلْنَا مَا لَا طَاقَةَ لَنَا بِهِ وَاعْفُ عَنَّا وَاغْفِرْ لَنَا وَارْحَمْنَا

SERDAR KILIC IS A LIFELONG STUDENT OF ISLAM AND ITS INTELLECTUAL HISTORY. HE ALSO STUDIES PHYSICS AND PHILOSOPHY AT THE UNIVERSITY OF VIRGINIA, WORKING TO SYNTHESIZE NEW IDEAS AND PERSPECTIVES.

# ONE GOD
## AND FATHER OF US ALL

### by The Rev. Anne McRae Wrede

From the deepest mists of time our Holy Scriptures tell of Abraham's wanderings through life with his wife Sarah from Mesopotamia, possibly near Edessa (Urfa in modern day Turkey), across the Sinai and into Egypt and then back again into the Hebron Valley. These Holy Scriptures also tell of Abraham's spiritual wanderings and even his stumbles, as he becomes ever more aware of the call to live in a covenant relationship of righteousness, trust and love with our *One God and Father of Us All.*

Like so many of us today, Abraham, this great and ancient archetype of so many faiths and cultures, was called into a personal relationship of righteousness and faith with God and humanity. Descriptions of the human experience as we struggle with both good and evil extend through his life and all through the genealogies of our faith for thousands of generations; the path of faith and righteousness, though life and culture are filled with both human weakness and yet also joy.

*The mausoleum of the Prophet Abraham in the city of Hebron.*

*Cave of the Patriarchs (Machpelah). According to the Bible, Abraham purchased the cave and the plot found in this spot to bury his wife Sarah. Muslims call it Ibrahimi Mosque.*

Christians take heart and great assurance in these accounts of the struggles and the enduring honesty, faithfulness and forgiveness shared between God, Abraham and Sarah. They are the ancestors of our Savior Jesus Christ, whom we believe has stepped into history to bring us forth in forgiveness and restoration from our own weakness and stumbles in our life of faith. So Christians also claim Abraham and Sarah as our own ancestors.

The Book of Genesis (25:9) tells us that when Abraham "was gathered to his people" his sons Isaac and Ishmael came together to bury his remains in the cave of Machpelah that was purchased earlier from the Hittites as a burial place for his wife Sarah.

I find this passage touched with love and hope for each of us today. For here we notice that Abraham's sons, who took their separate ways as patriarchs in their own expressions of faith, came together once again to honor their father. They came together in peace even in the presence of their mutual and ancient enemy, the Hittites.

And so, may we, as brothers and sisters in faith like Abraham, Sarah, Ishmael and Isaac, and even those beyond the understanding of our faith, be brought together again under the high calling of living within God's covenant of steadfast love, abiding justice and eternal mercy.

THE REV. ANNE MCRAE WREDE IS A PRIEST IN THE EPISCOPAL CHURCH USA.

# ISAAC AND ISHMAEL

## BELOVED OF ABRAHAM AND OF GOD

### by Rabbi Yakov Nagen

I am a Rabbi whose life work is healing the relationship between Judaism and Islam in the belief that there is a great story that we share and in which each have a place and a part. Formative to both of our traditions is the great faith and devotion of Abraham expressed in his willingness to sacrifice his son in submission to the will of God. Muslims commemorate this event on Eid al-Adha and Jews do so on Rosh Hashana, the Jewish new year. God is a God of mercy and love so that both versions of the story end in life and blessings, not in death.

The differences in the tradition should also be embraced and serve as a source of connection. In the Bible the son is Isaac whereas although the Qur'an doesn't explicitly designate the identity of the son, according to Islamic tradition the son was Ishmael. A close friend of mine is a Muslim Sheikh from Nazareth. When once asked who was the son in the story of the sacrifice, he replied "if it is Ishmael, it is my father. If it is Isaac, it is my uncle. Either way it is my family and family we must love and learn from." His words recalled to me the poignant scene in the Bible where Isaac and Ishmael come together to bury their beloved father.

My father-in-law, a professor of biblical studies, Uriel Simon, points out that in a close reading of the Bible there is truth in both traditions. Parallel to the story of Abraham being asked by God to sacrifice Isaac, the Bible tells the story of Hagar going into the desert with Ishmael. In that story too there is a danger of death as Hagar believes that Ishmael will die of thirst. There too at the last moment an angel from God comes to say that the son is spared, and there too the son receives great blessing. Genesis 21, 14-18 reads as follows:

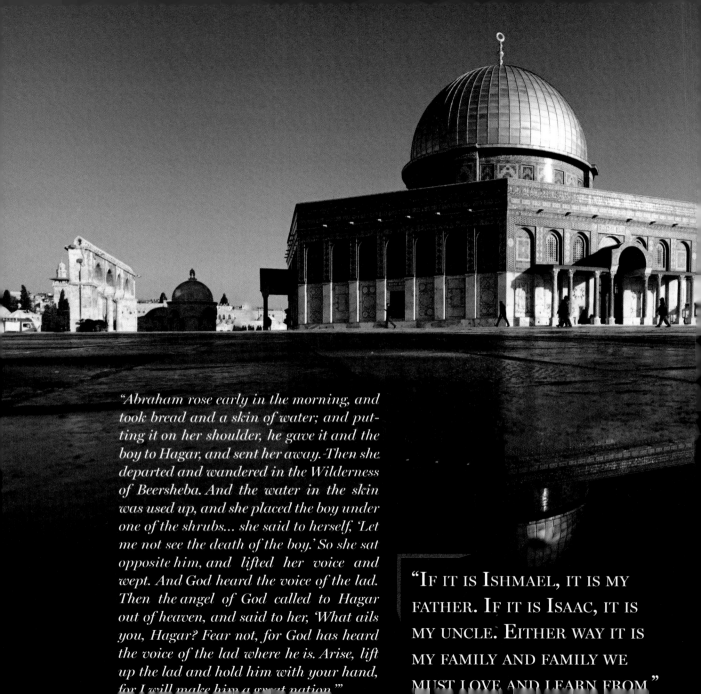

"Abraham rose early in the morning, and took bread and a skin of water; and putting it on her shoulder, he gave it and the boy to Hagar, and sent her away. Then she departed and wandered in the Wilderness of Beersheba. And the water in the skin was used up, and she placed the boy under one of the shrubs... she said to herself, 'Let me not see the death of the boy.' So she sat opposite him, and lifted her voice and wept. And God heard the voice of the lad. Then the angel of God called to Hagar out of heaven, and said to her, 'What ails you, Hagar? Fear not, for God has heard the voice of the lad where he is. Arise, lift up the lad and hold him with your hand, for I will make him a great nation.'"

"IF IT IS ISHMAEL, IT IS MY FATHER. IF IT IS ISAAC, IT IS MY UNCLE. EITHER WAY IT IS MY FAMILY AND FAMILY WE MUST LOVE AND LEARN FROM."

The great insight that Rabbi Jonathan Sacks derives from the parallels between the two biblical stories is that the Bible teaches that neither son, Isaac nor Ishmael, are rejected and that both are blessed. The is the message that Jews and Muslims must embrace. In my recent visit to the home of the beloved Hocaefendi Fethullah Gülen, I saw in his room the picture of the verse from the Qur'an (4:125), "Abraham is the beloved friend of God." Abraham loves both of his children and all of their descendants. As God loves Abraham, He loves all of Abraham's children.

The very name of the recent peace agreements between Israel and the Arab nations symbolizes a paradigm shift. As opposed to previous accords, Camp David and Oslo which are named after locations foreign to the Middle East, the "Abraham Accords" expresses the shared religious heritage uniting Jews and Muslims. If religious identity was once a wedge dividing Jews and Muslims, here it is being channeled to create a narrative of connection.

Perhaps we should take this language one step further and call future peace agreements, the Isaac and Ishmael accords!

Ultimately, the goal goes beyond the Middle East, beyond Jews, and Muslims. We must join together to return to the first father and mother, Adam and Eve to create global respect and brotherhood for all humanity. The Talmud teaches that this is why God chose to limit creation to begin with one common ancestor for all (Sanhedrin 37a).

If in the so much conflicted Middle East we find the path for reconciliation and connection through our common roots, this can give hope and direction for our broken world to build a joint future for all.

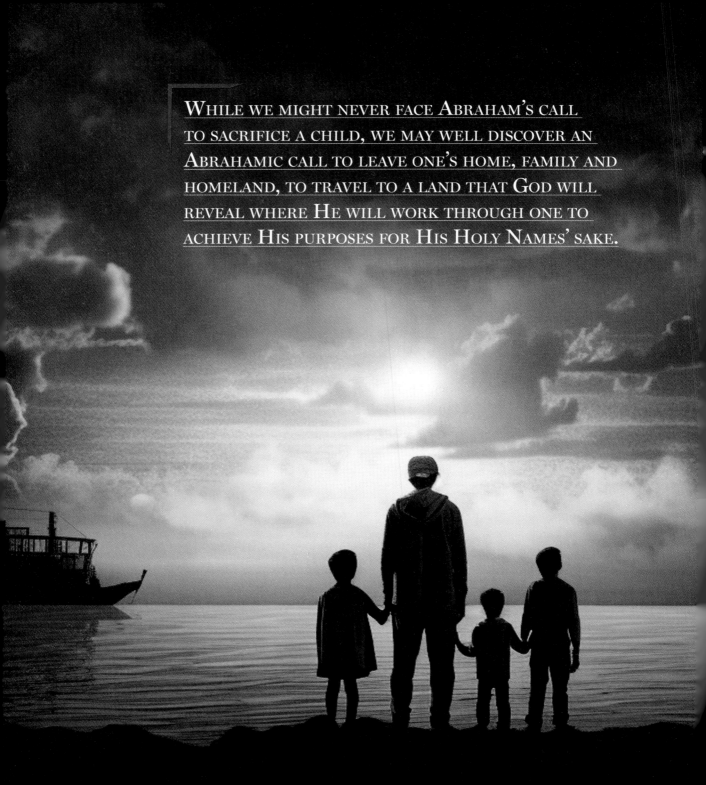

WHILE WE MIGHT NEVER FACE ABRAHAM'S CALL TO SACRIFICE A CHILD, WE MAY WELL DISCOVER AN ABRAHAMIC CALL TO LEAVE ONE'S HOME, FAMILY AND HOMELAND, TO TRAVEL TO A LAND THAT GOD WILL REVEAL WHERE HE WILL WORK THROUGH ONE TO ACHIEVE HIS PURPOSES FOR HIS HOLY NAMES' SAKE.

# THE SACRIFICE OF OBEDIENCE

## A PERSONAL MEDITATION

### by Daniel Skubik

Abraham's faithful response to God's call to sacrifice his son is an ancient narrative shared by all Abrahamic faith traditions. As such, it has birthed numerous interpretive understandings over the centuries, speaking to the concerns and needs of each successive faith generation. Sometimes these understandings arise from differences in details of the event presented across the revealed Scriptures. Yet most all focus on the terrible internal struggle of mind and spirit that must have engulfed the Patriarch as he prepared to obey, and the ultimate relief and subsequent blessing that flowed from his obedience when at the penultimate moment he was interrupted by the Angel of the Lord to stay his hand and so was able to substitute an animal sacrifice in place of his son. For such giftedness of faithful obedience, believers today can rightly be thankful. And thus remembrances and celebrations—sharing the narrative and the blessing— continue to be the order of the day.

But let's focus for a moment on what is typically left unremarked by these commentators. That is, while Abraham was indeed obedient and blessed, his willingness to sacrifice his son was very costly nonetheless. Beyond any internal struggles he may have fought beforehand, what can we say about the internal and external consequences afterwards? For natural consequences there were, and apparently serious ones.

The Hebrew Scriptures provide interesting details that should not be overlooked when attempting to understand this episode and its consequences in the life of Abraham and his family. In particular, it is important to note where everyone was residing, for in fact—according to the narrative in Genesis—they are not all residing in the same place after the event. At the time of God's call, it seems the family were all in Beersheba, the place from which Abraham and his son set out. But after the events on the mount? Abraham is back in Beersheba (Genesis 22), but Sarah is in Hebron—a fair distance to the northeast (Genesis 23); and Isaac is discovered to be residing in the Negev in the region of Beer-Lahai-Roi (Genesis 24)—the well of Hagar from Genesis 16 and a significant distance to the southwest. How did this geographic dispersion come to pass? The scriptural narrative is silent, but let me offer the following meditation.

Obedience is costly. How much more so when one may need to explain oneself to one's family members. There is no direct indication in the narrative, for example, that Abraham ever explained to his wife what God had demanded and that he was going to obey; he just did it, leaving her to discover the facts of the affair afterwards. And when she did learn of the near death of her son, would she remain unmoved? Would she offer simple praise and thanksgiving? That she would fly from the presence of this man who came within a breath of taking her son's life and return to a place like Hebron which had once been a safe home seems the action of a most reasonable woman. Though the anguish also must have taken a toll on her health and well-being, for when we learn that she is in Hebron rather than Beersheba we also learn that she has died there. Abraham had to travel from Beersheba to mourn her and bury her.

Similarly, one can readily imagine a son's reticence to remain with a father who had just raised a butcher's cleaver to kill him. One might have expected him to decamp with his mother to Hebron. But perhaps he never returned to Beersheba with Abraham, instead escaping the mount and his father immediately for an oasis shared with Hagar and Ishmael, family members he could better trust. So in fact the narrative in Genesis suggests Abraham returns to Beersheba alone, and Isaac sees Abraham again only together with Ishmael after Abraham has died, when they come to bury him alongside Sarah in Hebron.

These last two proffered interpretive paragraphs are of course clearly speculative. As noted, there is nothing in any revealed text that details such a family breakdown and breakup. For all that, I do want to urge that such can be a very real cost of obedience to God's call. Indeed, that family can be experienced as

OBEDIENCE IS COSTLY. IT MAY BE THAT ONE PASSES THE TEST, ENABLED THROUGH GOD'S COMPASSIONATE MERCY AND UNLIMITED GRACE, AND RECEIVES THE BLESSING, THEREBY BECOMING A BLESSING.

hindrance rather than help toward obedience is a warning that can be drawn from many Biblical and Qur'anic passages. Such warning is explicitly expounded by several of the Hebrew prophets and in the Gospels, where Jesus warns that family members will be divided one from the other over him and his teaching. For example, in the book of Micah, the prophet declares that "a man's own household are his enemies"; and Jesus warns that brother will be against brother, father against child and children against parents, that the obedient will be hated by all.

Perhaps you are alone in your family regarding the importance of fasting and prayer during specific seasons like Yom Kippur, Lent, or Ramadan, and face opposition to adhering to that call. Or, you are among some who seek to undertake a pilgrimage, but to find the time and resources necessary is daunting, especially in the face of misunderstanding at home or incomprehension at school from classmates and teachers, or on the job from colleagues and bosses. Perhaps the struggle is to give more of one's limited time to prayer, meditation and thoughtful reading of one's scriptures and related texts, and so taking time away from "swimming" in social media's digital sea: a needful distancing from immediate gratification in today's modern world. The struggle is only compounded when it is easily misapprehended by others, who now accuse you of isolating yourself from family and friends, or even that you are merely engaged in "virtue signaling" and are attempting to make them feel guilty over their own screen time.

Moreover, while we might never face Abraham's call to sacrifice a child, we may well discover an Abrahamic call to leave one's home, family and homeland, to travel to a land that God will reveal where He will work through one to achieve His purposes for His Holy Names' sake. Or, mayhap one faces governmental or socially-based persecution of selected minorities, where division of households and disruption of extended families through imprisonment or banishment is all too common in these troublous times, and dangerous dispersion becomes unavoidable.

And so, *Deo volente*, it is for every believer, today. God still calls. Obedience is no less costly. It may be that one passes the test, enabled through His compassionate mercy and unlimited grace, and receives the blessing, thereby becoming a blessing. But costly consequences of a family's and others' misunderstanding or even incomprehension and opposition may remain. Yet, "whoever endures to the end will be saved" (Matthew 10:22).

DANIEL SKUBIK, PHD, IS A RETIRED PROFESSOR OF LAW, ETHICS, AND HUMANITIES.

"A SPECIAL SPARK RISES
FROM THE SORROW OF A
BURNING HEART.
HAVE YOU EVER HEARD
HOW THE SIGH OF A
BROKEN HEART
TOUCHES THE BELOVED?"
— RUMI

# TO BELIEVE AND "SACRIFICE"
## A SCIENTIFIC REASON

by Sumeyra Tosun

Throughout history, religion has, and continues to, occupy a powerful position in people's lives. Despite doubts raised by philosophers and scientists, religion has thrived in every culture for thousands of years with over 85 percent of the world's population currently subscribing to some form of religious belief. While this is so, there are many who are critical of religious traditions, especially with respect to certain rituals, which they find strange: fasting all day, going long distances to visit a sanctuary, circumambulating a building, and of course offering sacrifices are among such practices.

Many Islamic scholars have defined worship as submission to God with love and reverence and seeking nearness to Him by doing what He has commanded. Well, what is the place of such religious practices, which look strange to some, in our lives? How do we, as human beings, relate to the notion we call faith?

Neuroscience findings that have emerged in recent years show that we have a very fundamental relationship with faith – and therefore with such acts of worship. Researchers who explore the psychology and neuroscience of religion are shedding light on why, and how, religious belief endures. Neurotheologians contend that the human brain's structure and operation predispose us to have faith in God. They suggest that God's biological substrate is located in the limbic system, the brain's emotion center. According to Rhawn Joseph, a renowned neurotheologian, the limbic system contains "God neurons" and "God neurotransmitters" (Joseph, 2001). The hypothalamus, amygdala, and hippocampus are among the limbic structures that have been linked to religious conviction. Neurotheologians

WHAT IS THE PLACE OF SOME RELIGIOUS PRACTICES
IN OUR LIVES? HOW DO WE, AS HUMAN BEINGS,
RELATE TO THE NOTION WE CALL FAITH?

cite alterations in these regions in functional MRI scans of subjects practicing religious meditation. They argue that if thinking about God alters brain function, there must be an inherent neural drive to believe in God. A study published in 2009 demonstrated that religious thoughts activate the region of the brain involved in interpreting others' emotions and intentions known as "theory of mind" (Azar, 2010; Kapogiannis et al., 2009).

Thinking about God, it has been found, is akin to thinking about an authority figure, like one's parents. The difference is related to contemplative practices, such as meditation and prayer, which can alter the brain's wiring in regular practitioners (Slagter et al., 2011). When the brain activity of long-term Buddhist meditators was monitored during meditation with fMRI and EEG techniques, it has been found that they possess a more robust and well-organized attention system than novice meditators. Essentially, meditation, as well as other contemplative spiritual practices, improve attention and deactivates brain regions responsible for self-focus (Davidson & Lutz, 2008).

For the first time in history, we are gaining insight into spiritual experiences as not being separate from the human body but rather intertwined with human matter, specifically the brain's matter. Consequently, matter and spirit are no longer seen as opposing forces but rather as interconnected, if not identical (Delio, 2003).

Hamer's research does not aim to prove the existence of God, which falls within the purview of religion, but rather to demonstrate that spirituality is a genuine phenomenon that can be defined and measured. As Hamer views it, spirituality is rooted in genetics while religion derives from memes – the cultural equivalent of genes – ideas, values, or behavioral patterns passed from one generation to the next through non-genetic means, often by imitation. He posits that religion is influenced by environmental factors while spirituality is influenced by nature (Goldman, 2004; Hamer, 2005).

These cognitions share a common thread that leads us to perceive the world as deliberately designed by someone or something. Young children, for instance, often believe that even minor aspects of the natural world were created with a purpose. If you inquire why a collection of rocks is sharp, they may say, "So animals won't sit on them and break them." When asked about the reason for the existence of rivers, they may answer, "So we can go fishing" (Kelemen, 2004).

Research suggests that adults also tend to seek meaning particularly during times of uncertainty.

Neuroscientific studies lend credence to the notion that the brain has an innate inclination to believe. This inclination appears to be distributed throughout the brain and likely stems from neural pathways (Kapogiannis et al., 2009). This aligns with the Islamic principle of the "original pattern," which refers to the innate disposition that God has instilled in human beings. "So set your whole being upon the Religion as one of pure faith. This is the original pattern belonging to God on which He has originated humankind. No change can there be in God's creation. This is the upright, ever-true Religion, but most of the people do not know" (Qur'an 30:30).

Spiritual beliefs may also contribute to a longer and healthier life. A significant body of research indicates that religious individuals have a longer lifespan, are less prone to depression, are less likely to abuse drugs and alcohol, and are even more likely to attend dental appointments more regularly (Inzlicht & Tullett, 2010; 2011; McCullough & Willoughby, 2009).

Religion can also serve as a crucial tool for facilitating large, cooperative societies. The continued prevalence and importance of religion across cultures can largely be attributed to its use as a social mechanism. Religion is one of the primary methods by which societies encourage unrelated individuals to treat each other with kindness (Norenzayan et al., 2016). Research conducted in 15 diverse societies found that individuals who practiced a world religion displayed

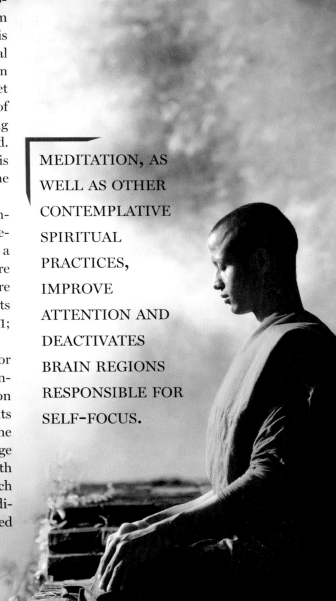

MEDITATION, AS WELL AS OTHER CONTEMPLATIVE SPIRITUAL PRACTICES, IMPROVE ATTENTION AND DEACTIVATES BRAIN REGIONS RESPONSIBLE FOR SELF-FOCUS.

greater fairness towards strangers in economic games than non-religious individuals (Henrich et al., 2010).

The Holy Qur'an emphasizes the importance of combining belief with good deeds, referring to true Muslims as "those who believe and do good deeds" (e.g., Qur'an 2:277; 4:173; 10:7, 10:23, 13:29; 19:93). Virtuous deeds serve as the guiding principle for Muslim behavior, and the concept of a "giving culture" is fundamental to comprehensive development in Islam. Therefore, there are various ways to promote charitable behavior and donations among Muslims. Sacrifice, or Qurban, is a significant method of charitable behavior in Islam. It involves sacrificing (usually) a sheep or a cow during a specific time of the year, and the Qur'an orders that the meat be eaten while also feeding the poor who live in *contentment and humility* (Qur'an 22:36). Muslims are prescribed to keep one-third of the share, and donate the remaining two. Although it is a demanding practice, many Muslims follow this order each year.

One of the primary purposes of the Qurban practice in Islam is to cultivate piety and increase believers' consciousness of God. As the Qur'an states, it is not the physical offering of the sacrificial animals that reaches God but rather the devotion and piety of the individuals who offer them (Qur'an 22:37). The practice is meant to bring believers closer to God and strengthen their relationship with Him as the word "Qurban" itself is derived from a root word meaning "closeness."

Overall, Islam emphasizes the importance of improving one's relationship with God and with all of His creation. The Qur'anic verses emphasize the significance of doing good deeds and being aware of God's presence in all aspects of life. This focus on piety and spiritual awareness may explain the prevalence of religious practices that promote prosocial behaviors, charitable giving among Muslims, and the relationship with our Maker. Thus, with the practice of sacrifice/*qurban* we fulfil our nature of being as we are predisposed to believe in God and develop a closer relationship with him.

## References

Azar, B. (2010). A reason to believe. *Monitor on Psychology, 41*(11), 53-56.

Davidson, R. J., & Lutz, A. (2008). Buddha's brain: Neuroplasticity and meditation [in the spotlight]. *IEEE signal processing magazine, 25*(1), 176-174.

Delio I. (2003). Are we wired for God? *New Theology Review, 16,* 31-43.

Goldman, M. A. (2004). *The God Gene: How Faith is Hardwired Into Our Genes.*

Hamer, D. H. (2005). *The God gene: How faith is hardwired into our genes.* Anchor.

Henrich, J., Ensminger, J., McElreath, R., Barr, A., Barrett, C., Bolyanatz, A., ... & Ziker, J. (2010). Markets, religion, community size, and the evolution of fairness and punishment. *Science, 327*(5972), 1480-1484.

Inzlicht, M., & Tullett, A. M. (2010). Reflecting on God: Religious primes can reduce neurophysiological response to errors. *Psychological Science, 21*(8), 1184-1190.

Inzlicht, M., Tullett, A. M., & Good, M. (2011). Existential neuroscience: a proximate explanation of religion as flexible meaning and palliative. *Religion, Brain & Behavior, 1*(3), 244-251.

Joseph R. (2001). The limbic system and the soul: evolution and the neuroanatomy of religious experience. *Zygon, 36,*105-136.

Kapogiannis, D., Barbey, A. K., Su, M., Zamboni, G., Krueger, F., & Grafman, J. (2009). Cognitive and neural foundations of religious belief. *Proceedings of the National Academy of Sciences of the United States of America, 106*(12), 4876-4881.

Kelemen, D. (2004). Are children "intuitive theists"? Reasoning about purpose and design in nature. *Psychological Science, 15*(5), 295-301.

McCullough, M. E., & Willoughby, B. L. (2009). Religion, self-regulation, and self-control: Associations, explanations, and implications. *Psychological Bulletin, 135*(1), 69.

Norenzayan, A., Shariff, A. F., Gervais, W. M., Willard, A. K., McNamara, R. A., Slingerland, E., & Henrich, J. (2016). The cultural evolution of prosocial religions. *Behavioral and Brain Sciences, 39,* e1.

Slagter, H. A., Davidson, R. J., & Lutz, A. (2011). Mental training as a tool in the neuroscientific study of brain and cognitive plasticity. *Frontiers in Human Neuroscience, 5,* 17.

SUMEYRA TOSUN, PHD, IS A PROFESSOR IN THE PSYCHOLOGY DEPARTMENT AT MEDGAR EVERS COLLEGE, CUNY.

THUS WE SHOWED
ABRAHAM THE DOMINION
OF THE HEAVENS AND THE
EARTH, THAT HE MIGHT
BE ONE OF THOSE WITH
CERTAINTY.

AL-AN'AM 6:75

ARTEM PRACTICED
PARACHUTING, LOVED THE
SKY AND FELT HAPPY IN IT.
WHEN FULL-SCALE WAR
BROKE OUT, HE RETURNED
TO THE FRONT.

# SACRIFICE FOR LIFE
## THE STORY OF ONE UKRAINIAN LULLABY

by Mariya Tytarenko

A mother sings her last lullaby to her son in a closed coffin. On June 21, 2022, the Lviv church is crowded, everyone is bidding farewell to the hero Artem Dymyd, who died defending his homeland in Russia's war against Ukraine three days ago. His mother Ivanka sings with a quivering voice: "Oh, my child, I will rock your lullaby, I will lay you down to sleep." The video of this lullaby will spread throughout the world. Ivanka will later say that during her song, her cry of pain and despair, reminiscent of giving birth to a child, she herself will be reborn. And then she will add: "The previous Ivanka is no more."

Like all his countrymen and women, Artem fought against invasion, rocket attacks, and filtration camps. At the highest price. The price of life. Artem did not live to see his 27th birthday by two weeks. A handsome, educated young man, full of life and joy, he was born in the family of Fr. Mykhaylo Dymyd, a Byzantine Catholic priest and the first rector of the Lviv Theological Academy (now the Ukrainian Catholic University), and noted iconographer Ivanka Krypyakevych-Dymyd, who besides Artem have 4 more children. Artem fought back in 2014, then traveled a lot and practiced parachuting, loved the sky and felt happy in it. When full-scale war broke out, he sold his Harley, bought a sniper rifle and military gear and returned to the front. The last thing he said before he died, severely wounded by shrapnel, bleeding, with both legs clamped with tourniquets: "I survived, I survived."

"A person's last words are his testament," says Ivanka. She took the long and hard path from complete apathy and rebellion against God – to absolute rebirth with an even stronger faith in her heart. "For God there are no living or dead," she says in dozens of different interviews, carrying the light of faith. "We are just learning to perceive our son differently. We live in the reality of the resurrected Jesus. And Artem, who is waiting for his resurrection."

For Ivanka, her son Artem is alive. She talks about him in the present tense, not in the past. "Death is the only way to pass into eternity," she says, wearing her son's yellow leather sniper gloves. From time to time, she wipes the tears that fall from under her glasses with them.

When Ivanka heard about her son's death, she felt a hole in her chest. She describes this feeling as if a sword cut off half of her body and she could see her arm and shoulder fell to the ground. The first nine days she lived on adrenaline. She rushed to provide aid and comfort in the hospi-

"OH, MY CHILD, I WILL ROCK YOUR LULLABY, I WILL LAY YOU DOWN TO SLEEP."

tal, washing blood, urine, brains, holding the hands of seriously injured soldiers. In this way she was helping her son. She also worked with children in a psychiatric clinic. Later, her inner resources ran out and for forty days she lay down in complete apathy toward the world. She remembers that it was not a disease, but a condition where the body was working just to breathe. It was her escape from grief and from reality. "Your son died, and you also have the right to die," she convinced herself. And then her younger son Dmytro, who has also been fighting in the war, called her and said: "Mom, get up!" His voice struck Ivanka like an electric current. Then she realized: "I have to get up now and go on with my life."

Ivanka began to look for support in her life. "You can't rely on dreams," she says, "dreams are quicksand." God became her comfort and support – "the truest reality, firmament." God is a gardener, says Ivanka, He sows seeds, and we water and take care of the sprouts ourselves. And God plucks the flower when it is ready. While saying this, Ivanka smiles, and then adds: "I will ask Artem what it's really like."

I look at Ivanka as God's miracle on this earth. As Abraham's sacrifice in today's world. I can share her pain as a mother, but I can never even come close to her Mount Moriah. In one of her interviews, Ivanka talks about Mary, who experienced her son's death on the cross, when he was hanging there nearly naked and tortured, and how Mary became the mother of many sons of the church there. Then she adds that after the death of Artem, many new sons appeared – among priests. However, she understood this only after she underwent her own sacrificial journey of her personal Calvary.

*Ivanka Krypyakevych-Dymyd, at the funeral of her son, Artem. June 21, 2022, the Garrison Church of Sts. Peter and Paul, Lviv, Ukraine. Photo courtesy of Mariya Varanytska*

AFTER THE DEATH OF ARTEM, MANY
NEW SONS APPEARED — AMONG PRIESTS.
HOWEVER, SHE UNDERSTOOD THIS
ONLY AFTER SHE UNDERWENT HER OWN
SACRIFICIAL JOURNEY OF HER PERSONAL
CALVARY.

*Dymyd family. Artem is wearing a blue emboidery.*

*365 steps of Calvary to reach the Church of the Virgin of the Angels (patron saint of Pollença)*

Ivanka is convinced that it is impossible to rejoice and sing "Hallelujah" immediately in grief, that there must be a rebellion against God. In her rebellion, she did not go to mass for a month. She asked God: "Where were you when my son was shot? After all, he is only 26, not even at the point of half his life yet. Do you need such a sacrifice, Lord? Bucha, Mariupol, Azov? The tortured, captured, killed? Why?" Now she says that she does not try to understand the ways of the Lord: "I ask only one thing – a drop of wisdom so that I can see the beauty of the path of my children."

In the Ukrainian tradition, there is a saying "Heroes never die." They would live in our memories and hearts. When Ivanka sang the last lullaby to her son lying in a coffin, she radiated conscious Abrahamic sacrifice in obedience to God, along with a new light of true faith. A light you can hold onto like the strongest lifeline. It can be worn like armor. With this light we will fight against evil, as though with a sword, until the very end. Because this is the sacrifice of the warriors of light. And their mothers. It is a sacrifice for life.

MARIYA TYTARENKO, PHD, IS AN ACCOMPLISHED AUTHOR WITH MANY AWARDS. SHE IS A PROFESSOR AT THE UKRAINIAN CATHOLIC UNIVERSITY, SCHOOL OF JOURNALISM AND COMMUNICATIONS.

# ABRAHAM
## A STORY OF TRUE SUBMISSION

by Hakan Yesilova

Imagine a situation where you have no choice but have to sacrifice your only child – your precious, who came late in your life as a great surprise.

Or think of yourself rejected by your father and your community because of your out-of-the-box beliefs that challenged theirs, and you have only a few who believe in you.

And just for good measure, add to these the wrath of the ruthless ruler of your land who has declared you his archenemy.

This would be more or less a very brief summary of the story of the great patriarch Abraham, peace be upon him, as told in the holy scriptures. Considered as one of the key figures in the history of monotheism, Abraham holds a very central role in the Jewish, Christian, and Muslim traditions. Today, his mission is being revitalized through interfaith meetings and panels where his legacy is discussed from the perspectives of different traditions, in the hopes of creating friendships across faiths. I had the opportunity of participating in some of these events in recent years and, while making new friends, I have also been able to see *my* Abraham in the eyes of friends from *other* traditions. At a time when we are challenged by polarizations, it is hope-inspiring to see many communities striving to build bridges and treating diversity as a source of richness.

What you will be reading below is an effort to share some reflections on this great man, whose life can by no means be retold within the limited scope of an article.

## Abraham in the Muslim neighborhood

Abraham (Ibrahim in Arabic and Turkish) is a commonplace name of Muslim cultural makeup, as many of our religious values are. Abraham and his family are remembered, praised, and prayed for by Muslims in their daily prescribed prayers, during the annual festival of sacrifice (*eid al-adha*), and also when performing the Hajj, which is the pilgrimage to the holy land of Mecca.

"Abraham" is a popular name across Muslim communities. And especially in places like Urfa, Turkey, Halil and Ibrahim are the most common names given to boys. "Halil" literally means friend and is one of the distinctive attributes of Abraham.

The historical city of Urfa, on the Turkish-Syrian border, is dedicated almost entirely to the memory of Abraham. Balıklı Göl, or Abraham's Pool, one of the most visited ancient sites in this city, is believed to be the place where he was thrown into fire, and by God's will, the fire turned "cool and peaceful" for him. According to the legend, the logs that were used in the furnace turned to fish, which still exist today.

Many restaurants across Turkey have the name "Halil Ibrahim Sofrası," which is an allusion to the generous hospitality Abraham used to show his

*Abraham holds a very central role in the Jewish, Christian, and Muslim traditions. Today, his mission is being revitalized through interfaith meetings. Top: Clergy and representatives from Jewish, Christian, and Muslim communities at an interfaith prayer event at Congregation B'nai Israel in Emerson, New Jersey. Bottom: Congregation B'nai Israel members visited Boshniak American Mosque in Elmwood Park, NJ.*

guests. In Turkish folk culture, it is told that he would not eat without having a guest at his table, and if there was no one, he would go out to find one.

## Stories attributed to Abraham

Some of the moral stories recorded in religious literature and discussed in reading circles are believed to have been first told in the scriptures that were revealed to Abraham. Prominent Islamic scholar Bediüzzaman Said Nursi noted that the story he narrates and expounds on in his 8th Word in the *Risale-i Nur* collection did originally exist in the "scrolls" of Abraham. Also told as an "Eastern fable" by famous novelist Leo Tolstoy in his *Confession* (1884), Bediüzzaman paraphrased this story for the purpose of his religious wisdom, turning the "traveler" in the story into two brothers, one obedient and wise and the other rebellious. In Bediüzzaman's version, the two brothers aim to reach the same destination but choose different paths; and as they go along, they are both challenged by the same ordeals (like escaping from a beast and trying to survive in a well); the way they respond to these challenges are indicative of their character and choices.

Bediüzzaman's version reads like a lesson on the fate of two characters, the wicked and the prosperous, in the *al-A'la* Chapter of the Qur'an. This parable is recorded as "Man in Well" in the legend of two Christian martyrs from India, Barlaam and Josaphat, and in other earlier versions in Buddhist literature, too (Bilici 2014). Joseph Jacobs wrote that this parable "was one of the most popular morals of mediaeval sermonisers. Indeed, it puts in a most vivid form the most central practical doctrine of both Christian and Buddhistic Ethics. The supreme attraction of the pleasures of the senses amidst all the dangers of life and the perpetual threat of death has never been more vividly expressed" (Jacobs, 1896, p. lxx).

As we have no access to the scrolls of Abraham, we cannot prove whether such stories originally date back to him or not. However, considering the widespread existence of this parable across different traditions, if we are to credit it to a historical figure, Abraham is certainly the best fit.

Another story attributed to Abraham goes that he was once again hosting a guest. As he started eating, he called the name of God first, while his guest did not. Abraham asked him why he did not say God's name first, to which his guest replied that he was a fire-worshipper. Abraham showed the man the door. Then, God asked Abraham why he did so. "He denied You, my Lord." God said, "That man has been denying Me his entire life, and I am still feeding him."

Whether this really took place as it is told here or not, the story reflects the infinite Mercy that rules the universe. God extends His mercy without questioning whether we truly recognize Him, and He asks us to do the same for others. This divine guidance is what lies behind Abraham's legendary hospitality, the one that finds expression in so many restaurant names today.

## Abraham, the friend of God

Islamic tradition records that God has sent every community a messenger to guide them to faith (Qur'an 10:47; 13:7). According to some narrations, there are as many as 124,000 messengers. Abraham, "the friend of God," is among the top five messengers of God, the others of whom are Noah, Moses, Jesus, and Muhammad, peace be upon them. They are called *"ulu'l azm,"* i.e. masters of determination, and are exclusively praised in the following verse from the Qur'an:

*Of the Religion (that He made for humankind and revealed through His Messengers throughout history), He has laid down for you as way of life what He willed to Noah, and that which We reveal to you, and what We willed to Abraham, and Moses, and Jesus, (commanding): "Establish the Religion, and do not divide into opposing groups concerning it." What you call people to is hard and distressful for those who associate partners with God. God chooses whom He wills and brings them together (in faith and in obedience) to Himself, and He guides to Himself whoever turns to Him in devotion. (42:13)*

*Some of the moral stories recorded in religious literature are believed to have been first told in the scriptures that were revealed to Abraham. The legend of two Christian martyrs recorded as "Man in Well" is one of those parables.*

## Abraham and Islamic worship

Practicing Muslims who pray five times a day mention Abraham's name at least 28 times (the number is double if one includes voluntary prayers) in the following way: "O God, send grace and honor to Muhammad and his family, just as You sent grace and honor to Abraham and his family." Many Muslims add Abraham's name to the prayer after eating when they ask for God to further His grace upon them (*ni'mat Jalil-ul'lah*), the Prophet's mediation on the Day of Judgment (*shafaat ya Rasulullah*), and the abundance God blessed Abraham with (*barakat Halil-ul'lah*).

A full chapter in the Qur'an is named after Abraham. A lengthy portion of this chapter (14:35-41) is a beautiful prayer of Abraham for Mecca to be a secure land and that his progeny to be protected from ever worshiping idols.

Abraham's legacy manifests itself more thoroughly in the pilgrimage to Mecca, which is an obligatory duty for Muslims who can afford it. Almost all of the rites of pilgrimage, the hajj, and the locations where the hajj is observed have all been inherited from Abraham. The history of Mecca, the holiest place for Muslims, starts with Abraham, when he brought his wife Hagar and baby son Ishmael to begin the first human settlement there. Muslims remember the frustration of Hagar seeking water as they run between Safa and Marwa around the holy sanctuary. As the pilgrims wash themselves from the well of Zamzam, they remember God's mercy upon her and upon humanity, when God sent them the angel to bring this abundant source of water from out of nowhere under Ishmael's heel; a fountain so abundant that it keeps flowing even today, watering pilgrims.

The Ka'ba, the cubic building located at the heart of Mecca, was built by Abraham and Ishmael. As Muslims circumambulate the Ka'ba, they start from the corner of Black Stone, which was placed by Abraham, and after their cycles are complete, they stand for prayer behind the Station of Abraham (*maqam Ibrahim*), which is believed to be the rock he climbed while building the sanctuary. Another rite of the hajj is Jamarat, where pilgrims throw pebbles at three pillars. It is believed that Abraham and his son stoned Satan away when he tried to seduce them to turn back from the sacrifice. And at Mina, pilgrims offer their sacrificial animals whose meat are given away in charity, as they remember Abraham's ordeal with his son, who God "ransomed with a sacrifice of tremendous worth" (Qur'an 37:107).

As a side note, a great majority of Islamic scholars agree that the son to be sacrificed was Ishmael, while some think he was Isaac. Whichever son was going to be sacrificed that day is not completely insignificant; however, there are more important lessons to be learned from this story, and it does not produce any benefit to engage in disputes on this matter. Besides, for Muslims, both Ishmael and Isaac are prophets and are equally respectable. This ordeal did not only testify to Abraham's and his son's incredible submission to God, but it also showed the atrocity of human sacrifice, which was, and unfortunately still is, one of the most violent forms of false devotion to the Divine.

### Abraham's mission

Islamic faith holds at its center the oneness of God, which is believed to be one of the key teachings of all prophets, from Adam to Muhammad, peace be upon them. Despite varying outward forms, all the messengers sent to humanity taught their communities God's uniqueness (*tawhid*), resurrection and life after death (*hashir*), messengership (*nubuwwa*), and worship (*ibada*). However, Abraham's firm stance against idolatry and other forms of associating partners with God (*shirk*), which had reached an unprecedented extreme in his time, made his mission even more connected to the revival of monotheism. Even when he was a child, he would not pay any respect to the idols his father was crafting. He always opposed his community's worshipping of idols and celestial structures, like the moon and the sun. While he was staunchly against them, he still engaged in a "gradual" effort to invigorate his audience's logi-

*As a part of the hajj rituals, Muslim pilgrims throw pebbles at three walls in Mina, near Mecca. It is believed that Abraham and his son stoned Satan away when he tried to seduce them to turn back from the sacrifice. Hundreds of thousands of pilgrims walk across a long stretch of land to perform this ritual (jamarat) during the first three days of Eid al-Adha.*

cal reasoning. The Qur'an explains, in 6:76-79, how their deities are temporary, even if they might be as bright as a star or as glorious as the sun, which are doomed to eventually set. Abraham voices the inner conscience of every human whose desire for eternity cannot be truly satisfied by false deities when he says, "I love not the things that set" (6:76). Professor Ibrahim Canan notes that Abraham's evident challenge to his own people "must have taken place after he had been thrown into the fire," when an intellectual struggle ceased to be possible (Canan 2007, 47).

Despite his gradual and convincing argument to inculcate certainty of faith, the response he got from his community was what almost all messengers of God received:

*We had showed Abraham (the ugliness and irrationality of polytheism and) the inner dimension of (the existence of) the heavens and the earth, and the eternal truth. We had done so that he might be one of those who have achieved certainty of faith (6:75). They replied: "But we found our forefathers doing the same" (26:74).*

Abraham's mission almost exactly matches the Prophet Muhammad's. Between them are connections at multiple levels: ancestral relations through Ishmael, the Ka'ba as the shared sanctuary, and their struggle to show the truth at times when idol-worshipping was at its highest. Leaving behind his hometown where idol-worshipping was the unbreakable norm, Abraham was ordered to build the Ka'ba, to be a direction for prayer and site of pilgrimage, as a place to praise the only true God the Creator. The Prophet Muhammad was born in the shade of this holy sanctuary, but it was already filled with hundreds of idols, and his mission was to reinstate its holiness by purifying it from them. Not surprisingly, when he started calling his community to the One God, they said: "Enough for us (are the ways) that we found our forefathers on" (5:104).

Another interesting connection is that the Prophet was a descendant of Ishmael, whose mother, Hagar, was given by the ruler of Egypt as a gift to Sarah, who gave her to Abraham. Centuries later, Muqawqis, the ruler of Egypt, would send Maria to the Prophet as a gift, and the Prophet would name his son from her Ibrahim, or Abraham.

## Submission

What stands tallest amongst Abraham's many virtues is his confidence in, and submission to, the Almighty. It is told that an angel came to offer help when Abraham was being thrown to the fire, and Abraham said, "Sufficient for me is God." He was in such a state of Divine refuge that he did not ask for the intervention of any other being.

Abraham's trust in God was also proven when he was told to take Hagar and his son Ishmael away from home and leave them in the middle of the desert. Abraham did not answer Hagar's questions about why he was leaving them there, until Hagar asked whether this was a command from God. The wisdom of this would manifest itself in time: Abraham and Ishmael would later build the Ka'ba there, and the Arab nation would emerge from that community. The Prophet Muhammad, peace be upon him, would come from that community, generations later.

Another ordeal Abraham had to face was sacrificing his son. It is told that when Abraham had the dream, he waited for two more days, and when he saw the dream again, he was assured of the Divine source of it. Both he and his son had full confidence in this command, and they were rewarded when God ransomed the boy and granted us the "festival of sacrifice," which we still celebrate today as we honor human life while sharing food with the poor.

***

Abraham's story is a rich source of lessons for anyone who seeks a life of virtue and commitment to a Prophetic mission. More importantly, as we are living through difficult times of extreme polarization across religious, cultural, and political divides, Abraham can be held up as a unifying figure among Jews, Christians, and Muslims, whose scriptures praise him and his family as the father of all prophets. His path of full confidence in God in the face of imminent death and apparently unbearable ordeals could inspire all of us today. It is especially useful for those being persecuted, forced to leave their homelands, abandon their families, and those threatened with torture and death.

## References

Bediüzzaman Said Nursi. 2006. *The Words*. NJ: Tughra Books.

Joseph Jacobs. 1896. *Barlaam and Josaphat: English Lives of Buddha*, London: Davit Nutt.

Leo Tolstoy. 1983. *Confession* (Translated by David Patterson). WW Norton & Company, NY and London.

Ibrahim Canan. 2007. *The Message of Abraham: His Life, Virtues, and Mission*. NJ: The Light, Inc.

Mücahit Bilici. 2014. "Kuyudaki Adam: Tolstoy, Bediüzzaman ve Buda." Istanbul: *Taraf*.

HAKAN YESILOVA IS THE EDITOR OF *THE FOUNTAIN*, A BIMONTHLY MAGAZINE ON LIFE,

"SUFFICIENT FOR ME IS GOD."

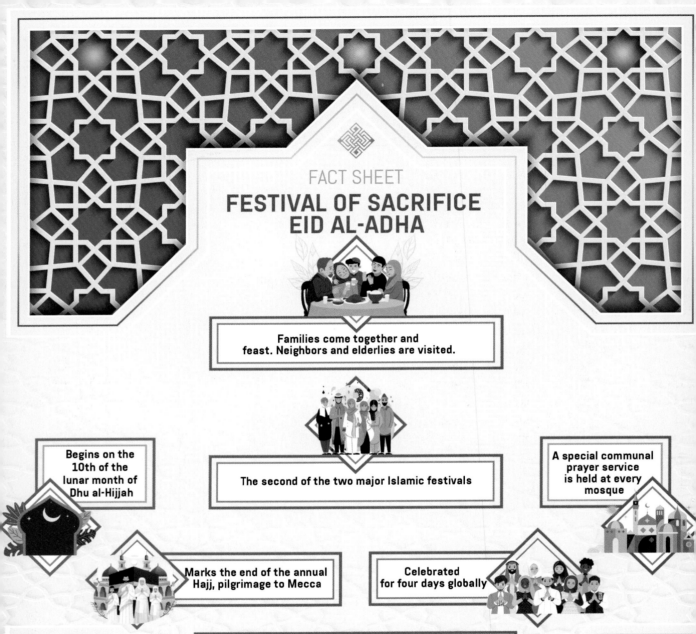

FACT SHEET

# FESTIVAL OF SACRIFICE
# EID AL-ADHA

Families come together and
feast. Neighbors and elderlies are visited.

The second of the two major Islamic festivals

Begins on the
10th of the
lunar month of
Dhu al-Hijjah

A special communal
prayer service
is held at every
mosque

Marks the end of the annual
Hajj, pilgrimage to Mecca

Celebrated
for four days globally

Those who can afford sacrifice a sheep (goat, cow, etc.)
and give away its meat in memory of Abraham and his son.